WHEN WE
ARISE
&
SHINE

God's freeing
vision for people
of faith

Keith Carroll

RIVER BIRCH PRESS

Mesa, Arizona

When We Arise and Shine
by Keith Carroll
© 2024 Keith Carroll

ISBN   978-1-956365-80-1 print
       978-1-956365-81-8 e-book

For Worldwide Distribution
Printed in the U.S.A.

River Birch Press
P.O. Box 7341, Mesa, AZ 85216

Table of Contents

Introduction   *v*

1. Resurrection Life   *1*

2. Come Up Higher   *7*

3. Arise and Walk   *13*

4. Faith Pursues Vision   *19*

5. God's First Nation   *26*

6. Second Call to Faith   *33*

7. Third Delivering Call   *40*

8. Visionary People   *47*

9. Full of God's Glory   *53*

10. Here or Yet To Come   *60*

11. End of Days   *67*

12. Our Last Times   *73*

Introduction

A lot is said and written about God's will and intention for us as individuals. While the ongoing purpose for our personal salvation is extremely important, God declared He has an enlarged purpose for gatherings of people of faith.

There is strength in numbers! It is imperative that we respond to God's call for unity and community. It is essential that we all fulfill our responsibility to be involved in the process of selecting our leaders. Remember the often repeated saying, "The only thing necessary for the triumph of evil is for good men to do nothing."

God appeals to us as groups and nations. He invites us to arise and respond to His guidance as free people. The Old and New Testaments relate how His first and renewed calls and delivering activities became historical realities.

Little is known or understood today about the prophesied third freeing call to faith in His guidance. It includes a release from this world's two-class enslavements.

This detailed analysis of God's three historic calls to faith may surprise you and cause you to rethink your position on the issues of the day.

Through *When We Arise & Shine*, you will be enlightened and inspired, so you can more purposely arise and shine in this day!

1

Resurrection Life

During the Easter season, many celebrate the resurrection of Jesus Christ. And rightly so, for resurrection demonstrates the amazing truth that our life involves more than natural experiences.

Our Bible and millions of recorded near-death experiences confirm our consciousness continues beyond this life. Scripture notes that our personal last day on the earth is *"in a moment,"* we *"in the twinkling of an eye…are raised incorruptible."*[(a)]

Clearly, God has much more in store for us: *"Things which eye has not seen and ear has not heard, and which have not entered the heart of man, all that God has prepared for those who love Him."*[(b)] While these verses speak of life in eternity, they also apply to a quality of life God offers us during the twinkling of our natural eye. And so we ask, what is resurrection life?

Arising From Inactivity

The word *resurrection* appears in our Bible thirty-nine times and only in the New Testament. It is translated from the Greek *anastasis*, which means: to arise, get up. It is a contrast to falling or remaining inactive. Resurrection is widely acknowledged as a rising out of the limitations of this natural life.

Jesus even applied it to life in this world: *"I am* (currently and for all time) *the resurrection and the life* (zoe – spirit life)."[c] *The Message Bible* translates it this way: *"You don't have to wait for the end. I am, right now, resurrection and life."* What is the resurrection Jesus spoke of?

The Bible notes God warning at mankind's beginnings: *"For in the day that you eat from it you will surely die."*[d] The Hebrew wording of Scripture actually says: *"For in the time that you eat from it you will be dying."* Rather than an immediate or eventual death, the sin would cause an ongoing deathly condition. Jesus later spoke of this reality by saying: *"Allow the dead to bury their own dead."*[e]

The original sin in the Garden of Eden was the act of ignoring God's input and breaking intimate interaction with our eternal Father. All sinful activity is a consequence of the first actions, which were in contrast to God's insightful and purposeful guidance. The story Jesus shared of the Prodigal Son also illustrates a picture of life apart from God's insightful guidance.[f]

Rebirth

Our spiritual life (*zoe*) is not just reserved for eternity. When we ignore God's input and only rely on the natural realm's *"good* (productive) *and evil* (destructive)" processes,[g] we shortchange the quality of life that God's presence makes available to us during this natural life.

For: *"While we are dead in our transgressions, Christ comes to us as a savior."*[h] Scripture even declares: *"This is eternal life; that they may know* (by experience) *Thee and Jesus Christ."*[i] When we partake of the spiritual life God offers, we rise from our relational sleepy slumber and experience a resurrection. As we receive from God's presence, we become more godly minded people.

While Scripture often refers to resurrection as happening after we physically die (our last day), it also speaks of us arising out of our inactive perceptions and deadly sleep-like conditions. We want to realize that God does not intend for us to wait until we die to experience resurrection life.

Our first stage of life is in a mother's womb where we are first formed and prepared for the enlarged experience of this world. Much like the first stage, this life is a preparation for the next. Our experience in this temporary world is preparing us for life in the enlarged eternal realm. We can, however, experience elements of eternal life in this world as a precursor to the next life.

A "birth from above" [j] awakens our consciousness and energizes us to the ever-abiding presence of God. A rebirth raises our conscious awareness and invites our intimate interaction with our Eternal Father. This is the influencing reign of God's Kingdom in our lives. As we awaken from spiritual inactivity, we receive a better understanding of God's intention for our life.

Our transformation into more spiritually minded people, [k] helps us become better expressions of God's Love and Light. [l] Scripture encourages us to *"Arise, shine; for your light has come, and the glory of the Lord has risen upon you."* [m] How amazing is it that God invites us to partake of His abiding presence?

Arise With Christ

The resurrection of Jesus included the natural body, to illustrate to all that he was-is alive. The anointed man Jesus was transformed to appear as a Spirit Being, to abide with us as a presence. He is able to come to us with the same look as before, with a different look, and as a spiritual presence. [n]

4

Scripture declares:

> *You were dead in your trespasses and sins in which you formerly walked...God being rich in mercy...even when we were dead in our transgressions, made us alive together with Christ...and raised us up with Him, and seated us with Him in the heavenly places.*[o]

While we live in this world, God provides a quality of life that originates from above. He invites or mind's comprehensions and the expressions of our heart to rise from this world's deathly ways: *"Arise, shine; for your light has come...the glory of the Lord has risen upon you."*[p]

Everyone can rise into a more heavenly mindset. For God has *"made us alive together...and seated us...in the heavenly places, in Christ."*[q] When we are open to the insights and eternal perspectives God shares, we can daily arise and live in more heavenly places.

Our repentant attitude allows God to assist our delivering release from bad attitudes and patterns of behavior. We can mature into better images and likenesses (reflections and resemblances) of God's heart,[r] and live by the eternal (ongoing) insights and perspectives He shares with us.[s]

The extent to which we experience resurrection life today depends on how fully we interact with

God-in-Christ. This is true for us as individuals and as families, communities, and nations. So why wait? Let's arise and partake of more resurrection life today and live above the fray of this temporary life.

"You don't have to wait for the end (death to time), *I am, right now, Resurrection and Life."*[t]

a) 1 Corinthians 15:2; b) 1 Corinthians 16:9; c) John 11:23-25; d) Genesis 3:6; 1 John 2:16-17; Romans 5:12; e) Matthew 8:22; Luke 9:60; f) Luke 15:11-22; g) Genesis 2:17; h) Ephesians 1:3; 2:1-6; i) John 17:3, 6:47; 1 John 5:11; j) John 3:3, 7-8, 15; k) Romans 15:5; l) 1 John 1:5; 4:8; m) Ephesians 5:14; Isaiah 60:1; n) Luke 24:15-15, 31; Acts 26:15; o) Ephesians 2:5-6; p) Isaiah 60:1; q) Ephesians 2:5-6; r) 2 Corinthians 3:18; s) John 12:49; 6:63, 68; 8:47, 51, 54-55; t) John 11:25 – *The Message* version

2

Come Up Higher

Are we listening, hearing, and discerning what God is saying to us as members of His family and as members of His responding children? God has a purpose for us in this earth.

God's design for our earthly journey includes a renewing richness we can know day by day! If we are not continually learning and growing, we can miss some of the benefits of our salvation.

Yes, God has more for us to know and experience when we die and leave this natural realm.[a] However, He invites us to know and experience some of the elevated perceptions and concepts of an eternal quality of life, while we live in this world. God invites us to come up higher—He has more for us today!

Delivered To Live Free

When God delivered ancient Israel out of slavery, He led them into a wilderness for a time of uncertainty.[b] The two-year short journey was to help them realize He was with them as their guide and to help them become confident that His purpose for us is much more than deliverance.

The delivered people needed to let go of the perceptions they learned under the enslaving care of overlords. God gave them time to accept the new concepts of freedom under His instruction. Deliverance was just a beginning that was intended to lead them into a productive life.

After experiencing two years of God's enlightening insight and miraculous care, the warless security of enslavement still appeared to be valued. Rather than rising to the challenges ahead and entering the blessings of the new life, they considered returning to a life of servitude.[c]

Since they were not willing to press into the abundant provision that was theirs for the taking, the delivered people lived the rest of their lives in an unproductive wilderness. Failing to enjoy the provisions God offered, they died in their fruitless lifestyle, void of the available abundance.[d]

Yes, deliverance was great, and God continued to bless and supply their natural needs during their time of reluctance,[e] but there was so much more available! The salvation God provides is more than a one-step or one-time experience. Our initial deliverance gives us opportunities to live free of this world's restricting perceptions and controls.

Waiting or Growing?

Are we maintaining the first ideas we were taught about God and this life? Have we let the teachings of educators, who were taught by their elders, settle into being our own perceptions? Can old views be holding us captive and keeping us from rising into the richness God is revealing for our day?

When we first believe and accept God-in-Christ, we are encouraged to simply acknowledge Him. A few changes in our attitude and outlook began to happen and give greater meaning to life. These beginnings are intended to help us transform perceptions and elevate our experience.[f]

Too often we are told Jesus will come in a future time to change our circumstances and make us more like him, as if we are to be satisfied with our unproductive wilderness and remain inactive. One verse appears to confirm such: *"They that 'wait' upon the Lord shall renew their strength; they shall mount up with wings as eagles; they shall run, and not be weary; and they shall walk, and not faint."*[g] The Hebrew word translated "wait" in this verse actually means "to bind."

This verse is really declaring that all who are tightly bound to God renew their strength and do

9

not get weary or faint. Our close communion with God produces an enduring strength, so we can continue to arise and move forward. While we don't want to proceed without God,[h] we do not want to settle for waiting and miss what He is providing.

When we are new to life under God's influencing governance, we tend to speak as a child.[i] After following Jesus for three years, the disciples were told there was more for them, but they were not ready to hear. Their earlier ideas of the ways of God and His Kingdom were still complicating their ability to perceive more.[j] The improving quality of life God offers can require that we let go of some of our early perceptions.

Following the resurrection and ascension of Jesus out of their natural sight, the disciples began to see Jesus as a presence of Spirit that immerses us in the Holy Spirit.[k] As they became more spiritually sensitive, they were able to hear and perceive what they were not able to previously receive.

A few years later, Paul, who was actively committed to the faith of his fathers, heard the voice of Jesus.[l] Paul then began to see and declare insights that Peter did not yet see.[m] We do not want to settle for where we are and be like the Israelites of old—unable to see and receive more.

God Has More

God still has more to say to each of us, in and for our day. We do not want to settle for what was revealed to the last generation, during the season of revivals and miracles, or for what we already know. While everything God has revealed in the past was good, He has more to say for our day!

Deliverance brings opportunity and a responsibility to grow in our perceptions and experience with God. He invites us to intimately know God-in-Christ, entertain His presence, and receive an ever-increasing quality of life in our day.[n] A more abundant life is ours for the taking!

"I came that you may have life, and have it abundantly."[o]

"As Christ was raised from the dead…so we too might walk in newness of life."[p]

God desires that we walk in newness of life today and not wait for a someday in the future. We can arise into new perceptions and understandings for our day. *"For this reason it says, 'Awake, sleeper, and arise from the dead* (our inactivity), *and Christ will shine on you.'"*[q]

Christ is the anointing of God that comes to deliver us from our deathly sleep (inactivity). *"Arise, shine; for your light has come…the glory of the Lord has risen upon you.*"[r]

Rather than wait, our conscious soul's mind, will, and emotions can *"lay aside the old self and be renewed…and put on the new self."*[s] We can experience an enlightening moment that *"makes us alive… and seats us in heavenly places."*[t] We can even soar daily "as eagles."[u]

Are we tightly connected to God? Do we find our strength is renewed, and we mount up as eagles? Let us be open to the process of arising into all that God's governing Kingdom influence desires for us. You can believe it; God has more for us in our times, in this day!

a) 1 Corinthians 16:9; b) Exodus 13:17; c) Numbers 14:1-4; Exodus 16:2-3; d) Deuteronomy 8:2-5; e) Deuteronomy 5:5-6; Joshua 5:11-12; f) Romans 12:2; Ephesians 4:24; 2 Corinthians 3:18; g) Isaiah 40:31; h) Numbers 14:39-45; i) 1 Corinthians 13:11; j) John 16:12; k) Acts 2:33; John 14:18, 23; l) Acts 9:5; 22:8; 26:15; m) Acts 11:2-18; n) John 17:3;o) John 10:10; p) Romans 6:4; q) Ephesians 5:14; r) Isaiah 60:1; s) Ephesians 4:20-24; t) Ephesians 2:4-6; 1:3; u) Isaiah 40:31

3

Arise and Walk

Ever since the sinful turn from God's guidance in the Garden of Eden, we are inclined to focus on the wisdom gained from natural experience.[a] We tend to believe and accept what our natural senses see and hear while we discount the insight our spiritual senses bring.[b]

What is the good news? Scripture says we can overcome our deathly attitudes and actually rise into better ways of living in our day. *"Christ was raised from the dead...so we too might walk in newness of life."*[c] So, how do we arise and walk in new life?

Learning To Arise

The spirit of life, which comes from our eternal Father, is in every living person and enables us to sense what the Spirit of God is saying and doing. We are invited to stop falling for the Garden's lie and repentantly rise into the fresh awareness and understanding God makes available.

Like resurrection (a standing up into fresh awareness), we can arise and advance into improving life experiences. While our circumstances may not immediately change, our improved attitude will produce an inner peace and levels of calming confidence to get up each day and do better.

We understand our physical body eventually declines, wears out, and returns to dust, while our spirit (breath of life) returns to its source, to God.[d] It is our conscious soul (mind, will, and emotion) that can understand what God is saying and doing, so we are renewed daily and arise into a clearer spiritual awareness.[e]

As we acknowledge our need for God's insightful wisdom and guidance, a repentant attitude restores us into the fellowship of His presence where we can partake of the Tree of Life—our source of spiritual (*zoe*) perceptions. As we see and hear more clearly, we arise to become better expressions of God's heart.[f]

While our physical health and well-being is always important to us and to God, more than our natural body, God is after the salvation of our conscious soul.[g] This is because what we think and feel in this life tends to infect our attitude and affect our actions for good and for bad.

Jesus lived "in" resurrection life (fellowship with

Father) and displayed the peace that passes natural understanding.[(h)] When Peter was released from his restrictive attitude toward non-Jews, he began to live above the separating mindset of his religious perception.[(i)] Biblical examples of people learning to arise, live, and walk with God's abiding and enabling presence are endless.

Understanding Spiritual Consciousness

The King James translators rendered eleven different Greek words into English simply as "life," hiding much meaning. Three of the Greek words specifically identify and address different aspects of life.

One Greek word is *bios*. It appears eleven times to address the temporal issues of natural life. Examples are: *"That prayers…made on behalf of all…that we may lead a tranquil and quiet* (natural) *life."*[(j)] *"The seed* (of God's life-giving word)…*are chocked with the worries, riches and pleasures of this* (natural) *life."*[(k)]

Another Greek word is *psuche*. This is used 101 times to speak to the issues of our soul's conscious mind, will, and emotion. Examples are: *"They are seeking my* (conscious) *life."*[(l)] *"Whoever wishes to save his* (conscious) *life shall lose it, but whoever loses his* (conscious) *life...shall save it.*"[m] Ideally, our conscious perceptions of this life are "transformed by the renewing of our mind." [n]

The Greek word *zoe* occurs 135 times to address the activity and quality of our spiritual life. Examples are: *"Jesus...brought* (spirit) *life and immortality to light.*"[o] *"I came that they might have* (spirit) *life and have it more abundantly."*[p] *"We have passed out of death into* (spirit) *life, because we love the brethren."*[q] The abundant use of zoe in Scripture amplifies the importance of our spiritual life and activity. When we interact with God, our spirit led life tends to improve.

The influence of our natural life (*bios*) is temporal and will eventually pass away as all things natural. The influence of our spiritual life (zoe) however is an ongoing factor.[r] It is our natural and spiritual experiences that feed and lend to developing our soul's conscious perceptions (*psuche*). While we appear to be more conscious of physical activity than spiritual, no one is totally void of a spiritual consciousness. We just tend to ignore it.

Planting Seeds

Everyone is invited to be *"born from above."*[s] What an amazing gift! We can rise out of our deathly slumber. A rebirth is to activate a conscious resurrection in this life. This opens us up to intimate interactions with our Eternal Father. Our communion with God allows us to receive eternal insights so we can consciously live above many of this life's restricting perceptions.

Some of these life-improving insights are listed in Scripture as fruit of the Spirit: *"But the fruit of the Spirit is love, joy, peace, patience, kindness, goodness, faithfulness, gentleness, self-control; against such things there is no law."*[t]

In nature, fruits are the sweet and fleshly products of a tree or other plants. Fruit is edible and usually quite pleasant. They contain a seed or several seeds that can reproduce more fruit. Scripture encourages us to *"taste and see that the Lord is good."*[u] For, *"as Christ was raised from the dead...we too might walk in newness of* (zoe-spirit) *life."* [v]

Additionally: *"That we might bear fruit for God... that we serve in newness of the spirit and not in oldness of the letter."*[w] Jesus prayed for those who arise into intimate fellowship with his eternal Father; *"As Thou didst send me into the world, I also have sent them."*[x]

As we arise and consciously walk in this better way of living, we partake of the many benefits of resurrection life. The fruits of the Spirit that we adopt as part of our own become heavenly attitudes, demeanors, expressions, and actions. These displays are observed by others and become invitations to join this inspiring life style. In time these seeds can produce the same fruit in their life.

Let's arise in resurrection life and share our enlightened way of living with others.

a) Genesis 3:6; 1 John 2:16-17; Romans 5:12; b) Psalms 34:8; Matthew 11:4-5; 13:16-17; c) Romans 6:4; 7:6; d) Ecclesiastes 12:7; e) John 10:10; f) John 17:3, 18; 3:16; g) Psalm 6:4; 119;81;1 Peter 1:9; h) John 1:4; Philippians 4:7-8; i) Acts 11:2-18; j) 1 Timothy 2:1-2; k) Luke 8:14; l) Romans 11:3-7; m) Matthew 16:25; 10:39; Luke 17:33; Mark 8:35; John 12:25; n) Romans 12:2; o) 2 Timothy 1:10; p) John 10:10; 5:40; q) 1 John 3:14 r) Ecclesiastes 12:7; s) John 3:3, 7-8, 15; t) Galatians 5:22-23; u) Psalm 34:8; v) Romans 6:4; w) Romans 7:4-6; x) John 17:18

4

Faith Pursues Vision

The biblical book of Proverbs is highly recognized for its profoundly wise sayings. One declaration says: *"Where there is no vision, the people perish* (KJV)."[a] This verse declares a common vision is the stabilizing value in interactive groups of people.

When gathered groups do not maintain a common vision for life beyond their individualities, they eventually divide and perish as *"a people."*[b] So we ask, why should people of faith pursue a vision beyond their personal welfare?

Understanding Visions

Visions provide viewpoints that can elevate our overall understanding of reality and improve our pursuit of a good life. Visions generally have an improving quality that helps us revise our earlier perceptions, overcome past experiences, labor through complications, and pursue improvements.

Visions are views and perceptions we can see, accept, pursue, ignore, forget, and even allow to die.

We receive visions in different ways. One way is a visual our inner eye sees that enables us to pursue a new reality. Another is a thought that drops into our consciousness and helps us perceive what we did not see before. Visions are inspiring moments that can improve the quality of our lives.

While we all seek what is good for us personally, a vision can inspire the creation of a new product, form a new service, or organize people for the benefit of the large group. Visions lend strength to the weak by connecting us to the activity of the group that is pursuing the vision. The Gospel good news is such a vision.

A vision can bring us together, improve our interaction, and elevate the quality of our activity. This reality is experienced in marriages, fellowships, nations, and commitments to God. When a vision is ignored, forgotten, or dismantled, the bonding strength in the gathering tends to fade away and eventually cease to be pursued.

Heavenly visions provide a unifying purpose that can help everyone work through the difficult "good and evil" activities of this world. By following God's lead and walking in His revealing light, we can overcome the back and forth swing of this world's "productive and destructive" forces.

God-Given Vision

The first vision God gave for mankind was given as He was creating the vast natural universe. As God's "image and likeness," they would be reflections and resemblances of His nature.[c] The earth was designed to be the place where God would birth, grow, teach, and develop His human offspring.[d]

As God formed the first one out of natural dust and infused it with His Spirit, He gifted the new personage with the ability to sense, communicate, and interact with both the natural and spiritual realms of reality, with heaven and earth. As the new being "became" aware, a conscious soul began developing.[e]

Then God took from the first to form a second, so their interaction would assist in the growth and development of His family.[f] Every living person has an infusion of the Spirit of God, which we tend to call the "spirit of life." Every child birthed into this life is an expression of God and man.[g]

Sadly, the first two chose to ignore the Eternal One and focus on the wisdom gained from the experience of nature's "good and evil."[h] It was their choice to ignore God that brought a death to their intimate fellowship with their Father. So, confusing perceptions of God began to develop. Failing to repent and adjust, their misperceptions took root, and they were removed from the Garden of God's presence.

Their sin did not negate their ability to hear God, for He came to them and their offspring, to offer insight about their "choices and attitudes." [i] We are all good and bad reflections and resemblances of the vision God gave; the image and likeness of His character, attitude, and personality (CAP).

Families are small examples of God's vision for gathering enlargements. They illustrate His functional purpose as we are a combination of different abilities, perceptions, and personalities. We partake of the present, are a result of the past, are involved in forming the future, and enlarge God's family.

Visions generally have a spiritual quality that helps us overcome many of this natural life's perceptions and limitations. The New Covenant vision of "Christ as God's Saving Presence" draws responders together to become larger illustrations of God's loving and embracing nature.

Visionary People

Jesus instructed us to *"follow Me"* [j] and respond to the Father "as you see me" respond. [k] This binds our differences together for a common cause and empowers us to do *"greater works."* [l] As we respond to God's influencing oversight and gather as groups, we become visible illustrations of His nature and way of life.

One of the most visible features of a heavenly vision is our love of God and one another. Our love is a reflection of God's love. Did you know God's love never ceases? [m] Oh yes, under the New Covenant, people of faith that function under God's guidance are called the *"Body of Christ."* [n]

Throughout history, many people have responded to God's insightful guidance. [o] While God has a vested interest in each person, He has illustrated a parallel purpose in our function as communities and nations. Scripture verifies God's interest in national affairs by saying: *"He sets up and brings down kings,"* and *"determines the times nations operate and sets their boundaries."* [p]

God even establishes nationhood for *"the sake of His people."* [q] Yes, God supernaturally intervenes in human affairs. He gathers many people into fellowships to respond to His influencing guidance while living in this natural world's good and evil atmosphere. God is also a gathering force for nations to function as larger witnesses of His reality and ways.

In many ways, America is an example of a godly vision for a nation under God. The nation offers a freeing liberty and justice for all. Such freedom provides opportunities for all to improve the quality of their spiritual and natural life. The American Dream is a vision that people gravitate to as they seek to live in freedom. Everyone can worship God according to the dictates of their heart. We can even pursue levels of prosperity as productive expressions of our eternal Father.

The Old and New Testaments give details of two times God has called people out of the enslaving two-class system, to live under His guidance as a free people. The Bible also tells of a third time when He would deliver people of faith into freedom under His care. We can draw much insight from these two examples and learn how to be better people and illustrations of His will for us as a people.

Visionary people are able to move beyond this world's perspectives and limitations. Our ability to be better images and likenesses of God improves as we are responsive to His influencing presence.

Stay tuned as we delve in the next chapter into the historical times when God has called people of faith to live under His guidance as a nation. Yes, our Bible tells of three! We will note insights and similarities in each call to function as "My People." Knowing our past is important, so we do not repeat its errors.

a) Proverbs 29:18; b) Matthew 12:25; c) Genesis 1:26; d) Genesis 1:1-30; e) Genesis 2:7; f) Genesis 2:18, 21-24; 4:1; Acts 17:22-27; g) Genesis 5:1-2; h) Genesis 3:6-7; 2 Corinthians 11:3; 2 Corinthians 11:3; i) Genesis 3:8-14; 4:6-7; j) Matthew 16:24; k) John 5:19; 13:15; l) John 14:12; m) Lamentations 11:12; Psalm 107:1; 1 Corinthians 13:4-8; n) 1 Corinthians 12:27; Romans 12:5; Ephesians 4:12; o) Isaiah 63:11; 2 Peter 1:21; p) Job 12:23; Daniel 2:21; q) 2 Samuel 5:12

5

God's First Nation

The eternal One created this natural universe and the unique planet we call earth, as a place to birth, grow, teach, and develop His offspring.[a] This would allow for growing and maturing processes for each person, for His collective family, and for all of humanity.[b]

Longing to see enlarged illustrations of His way of life in responsive children, God appeals to us as a gathering people and to us as nations.[c] God even establishes the vision of nationhood for *the sake of His people.*[d] So, what was God's first gathering vision for a nation?

A Delivering Invitation

God's first call for a people of faith to gather and function as a nation, was to Abraham's descendants and everyone living in slavery in Egypt. God selected Moses with all of his faults, mistakes, and shortcomings to function as His instrument, to be His visible savior.

There were many miraculous events to verify God's delivering invitation was real. Most of the slaves in Egypt gravitated to the vision of a life where they could be free to live and prosper. All who chose to believe in the promise of the God of Abraham and applied the blood of a lamb to their doorposts, were saved from the death messenger and became part of the people of faith.

Despite a common perception, the call was not just to the physical offspring of Abraham. Think about it—the Exodus was 400 years after Abraham first entered the land of Cannon[e] and four generations after Abraham's household of 70 people joined Joseph in Egypt.[f] In the Exodus, there were over 600,000 men of war age.[g] Counting one wife and just two children for each adult man, more than 2.5 million people responded to the call. Truly a mixed multitude!

The vision was for all people desiring to live free of the two-class system, under overlords.[h] All responding to the call became God's faith family, as offspring of Abraham.[i] God even called the mixed multitude delivered from slavery to live as a free nation, *"My son, My firstborn."*[j]

Responsibility of Freedom

The national vision obviously needed time to settle in. Their understanding of life as slaves under overlords who took care of them had to change. Their ingrained beliefs, desires, and attitudes would not allow them to responsibly function as free people. So God sent them on a two year journey.[k]

Fifty days after their deliverance in the first Pentecost, all the people heard God speak and invite them to personally interact with Him.[l] What a phenomenal event this must have been! However, almost without exception, in disbelief, the delivered people said they did not want to experience this again. Rather than personally interact with God, they appointed Moses to be their meditator, to stand between them and God's presence.[m]

During their journey, to verify they could trust this unseen God, He provided water out of a rock, bread-like manna in the morning, quail in the evening, and led them with a cloud during the day and a pillar of fire at night.[n] He even showed them they could be successful in battle.[o]

Despite personally seeing and partaking of all the miracles and hearing God speak to them, the people apparently chose to just perceive of God as their new provider. Since their faith as a people remained so elementary, their journey toward the productive benefits of freedom took forty years, a generation.

Actually, the delivered generation failed to become responsible believers. It was the children that grasped the full concept of faith, believing in God and having the will to pursue where He leads. When they grasped the concept of responsibly pursuing the vision God gave, they were able to enter, take possession, and enjoy the productive benefits of their salvation.

The territory was divided into thirteen areas or states. Interestingly enough, they functioned without a ruling upper class for 500 years by electing local elders and judges to mediate controversies.

While people refused to personally interact with God, they were still free of the stifling two-class system of servants and overlords. Much like today's middle class, they were free to live, worship, and prosper under God's oversight. The free nation flourished for several generations.

Although imperfect, the nation functioned and prospered as an illustration of a free society under God's oversight. God even made it clear, they were to welcome strangers and count them as natives born in the land if the strangers accepted and blended into the ways of the nation.[p]

Cycles Overlapping Cycles

When the free people decided to be like other nations and have a king, they invited the two-class system into the national experience. By choosing to submit to man's system of rule, they strayed from God's oversight and their freedoms began to slip away.[q] From that time on, the nation's prosperity and times of distress largely depended on the action and attitude of the ruling class.

Scripture reports that during their wilderness journey and after submitting to the two class system, *"this people has a stubborn and rebellious heart."*[r] They continually failed to heed God's caution, *"If you will…I will."*[s] The biblical record relates how every third generation came under oppression because the previous one *"failed to properly teach their children."*[t]

It was a vicious cycle. When an oppressed generation repented, they were delivered. Their children would grow up content and as comfortable people they failed to teach their own children about faith in God. The grandchildren grew up to be faithless and fell under the oppression of neighboring people. When they cried out for deliverance, freedom was restored. Then the cycle would repeat.

As a nation, they continually strayed from God's insightful guidance. When they forgot *"God their Savior"*[(u)] and His way of life, their prosperity stalled.[(v)] The nation continually failed to continually be God's influencing witness to the world, an example that would draw others into His way of life. God's firstborn nation eventually ceased to function and the people were dispersed.[(w)]

As we look at a short overview of cycles, keep in mind changes generally involve a process of beginnings and endings, with overlapping starts and stops.[(x)] Notice the 500 year cyclic responses to God's call; it was 1500 years after the first deliverance that He renewed the call.

2000 BC – Abram responds to God and becomes a father of faith.

1500 BC – God frees people to live under His guidance. Personal interaction is refused.

1000 BC – When people choose the two class system they begin to lose freedoms.

500 BC – The national experience ceases and people are dispersed.

00 AD – God-in-Christ renews God's call into fellowship with God's presence.

Our next chapter will look at the promised New

Covenant and view the history of God's second call to live as "a people" under His oversight. We will examine the overall response of those who accepted God's vision of living natural lives as spiritually minded people.

a) Genesis 1:1-30; b) Acts 17:22-25; 1 Timothy 4:10; c) Acts 17:26-29; Job 12:23; Daniel 2:21; d) 2 Samuel 5:12; e) Acts 7:6; Genesis 15:13; f) Exodus 1:5; g) Exodus 12:37-38; Numbers 1:44-46; h) Exodus 19:4-6; i) Romans 4:13-17; Galatians 3:6-9; j) Exodus 4:22-23; k) Exodus 13:17-18; l) Deuteronomy 4:10-12; 5:1-4; m) Deuteronomy 5: 22-27; Exodus 20:18-20; n) Exodus 17:6; 16:12-13; 31-35: 13:21-22; o) Exodus 17:8-13; p) Leviticus 19:33-34; q) 1 Samuel 8:6-8, 19-22;. r) Deuteronomy 9:6, 13; Jeremiah 5:23; s) Exodus 15:26; 19:4-6; t) Psalms 78:5-8; u) Psalm 106:21; v) Hebrews 8:9; w) Amos 9:8-9; x) Ezekiel 1:16; 10:10

6

Second Call to Faith

Before the first gathered people were scattered, God said He would make a New Covenant with people of faith.[a] The renewed call to faith in His oversight did not involve a place of separation and the Spirit of God would write *"His laws and ways in people's minds and hearts."*[b]

This call to faith would focus on what the first gathered people refused; personal interactions with our eternal Father. These people would respond to the abiding presence of God which would teach them how to really think, act, worship, and live natural lives as people of faith.

Second Delivering Call

Some 1500 years after the first visionary call and deliverance from slavery, God intervened a second time. By this time in history, the general perception of God's will for people of faith had deteriorated into a religion of rules and restrictions. The Jewish Torah contained over 600 laws.

The prophet Daniel declared: *"One like the son of man"*[c] would come to influence and oversee this faith response. He said this kingdom reality *"would never end or cease to be in the earth."*[(d)] This call came as a spiritual awakening, a rebirthing of God's vision for people of faith.

During this second call to faith, Jesus Christ proclaimed: *"The time is fulfilled and the kingdom of God* (His reigning presence) *is at hand* (within your reach), *repent and believe in the gospel* (good news)."* [(e)]

This declaration was to all: *"Whosoever will"* could partake and live as *"born again* (from above)."* [(f)] This kingdom experience was *"not coming with signs to be observed...behold the kingdom of God is in your midst,"*[(g)] in the middle of and between your interactions.

Jesus explained God's kingdom reign does not produce a utopian state or a perfect life condition; it is a developing reality *"full of mystery...a fruitful understanding...spreads like sowing seed...expands to affect everything...is a costly treasure...and can appeal to all."*[(h)]

While God's reigning oversight allows for *"tares among wheat"* and *"wolves among sheep,"*[(i)] our pursuit of the vision brings *"righteousness, peace, and joy."*[(j)] This reign was not coming by force, yet *"everyone is forcing his way into it."*[(k)]

As leaders of the old order opposed this unmanaged faith, Jesus announced the kingdom would *"be taken away from you, and given to a nation* (a people) *producing the fruit of it."*[1] Additionally, *"this generation"*[m] alive in that day would see it.

Paul confirmed the old was *"made obsolete…is ready to disappear."*[n] Those called the holy people were about to see their end time.[o] To illustrate the former was no longer relevant, the Holy City and Temple were destroyed in 70 AD.

"New Birth"

Jesus instructed people to *"Follow me* (my example)."*[p] He even prayed that followers would *"be with me where I am."*[q] Jesus asked that people would respond to God's insightful presence during this life, as He did. He desired that we follow God's guidance so we could live more *"abundantly."*[r] Responsive people are even called *"a nation producing the fruit of it."*[s]

Before the crucifixion, Jesus said, *"I will not leave you as orphans, I will come to you…and will disclose myself…and we* (my Father and I) *will come…and make our abode with you."*[t] After the resurrection, the "anointed man" they had known began appearing as "a spirit." This changed their perception of Jesus. God-in-Christ was now with them as an abiding presence of Spirit.

35

When Jesus ascended out of natural sight, He verified, *"I am with you always."*[(u)] As John the Baptist foretold,[(v)] on that Day of Pentecost, Jesus returned to baptize people in the presence of God's Spirit.[(w)] Now they could understand how Jesus would always be with them as a guiding and anointing presence. God's immersing presence became readily available; for it was *"poured forth upon all mankind."*[(x)]

Despite the overlords of the existing religious order, people of faith accepted the vision. Like airplanes that function and soar within the limitations of gravity, people of faith responded to the presence of God within the restrictions of their natural circumstances and various cultures.

People began relating to the abiding presence of God-in-Christ and to baptizing immersions in His presence.[(y)] Multitudes began to experience this *"new birth"* of awareness.[(z)] Responders became the *"Body of Christ,"*[(aa)] visible illustrations of God's abiding presence in the earth.

A Spiritual Awakening

This call to faith was a spiritual awakening and its reality really upset the world's concepts of God in a temple or on a shelf.[(bb)] This call to faith focused on personal fellowship with the abiding presence of God. Like the first call to faith, God spoke of this response as *"a holy nation."*[(cc)]

For over 300 years, people of faith proclaimed *"God is with us!"*[(dd)] God responds to our desire to be more like Jesus, as better expressions of our eternal Father's character, attitude, and personality (CAP). People became examples of God's love and light in their own communities.

While God did not have a problem with the different perceptions people developed, men began to try and congeal or standardize perceptions and practices of faith. Some began to promote the idea that there should be authorities over areas. A respected teacher of the day, Ignatius, taught, "We should follow a bishop as Jesus followed God, respect elders as apostles, and bring honor to bishops as unto God." Once again, a two-class system was introduced into the faith response.

In 313 AD, the converted Roman Emperor Constantine assembled area authorities into councils to form a standardized belief system. These councils continued to convene for over 200 years, arguing over what would be official doctrine. As decisions were decided, all other views and experiences were declared to be heresy. Like Israel of old, as leaders began to take control, freedoms began to slip away.

Eventually, worship of God apart from official beliefs and practices were forbidden. Within a few generations a veil seemed to come over the minds and hearts of people of faith as God's presence "with us" became a forgotten reality all over Europe and the Mediterranean regions. History confirms that in 500 AD, all sacred writings were removed from the public and the reading of Scripture was restricted to the ministry class.

Once again, people of faith fell under the control of overlords. This time it was a spiritual type of captivity. In this short overview of approximate dates, keep in mind that changes involve processes of beginnings and endings, with overlapping starts and stops.[ee]

1500 BC – God frees people out of slavery to live under His guidance, yet personal interaction is refused.

1000 BC – The people choose to be like other nations with a king and begin losing freedoms.

500 BC – The national experience ceases and the people were dispersed.

00 AD – God-in-Christ calls people into personal fellowship with the presence of God.

500 AD – Faith's response came under religious controls and sacred writings are withheld.

One religious system exercised control over public responses of faith for the next 1000 years.

We can learn much from these two historical calls to be "My people." Our next chapter shines light on God's third call to respond to His guidance and live free of the restrictive two-class system.

a) Jeremiah 31:31-34; b) Hebrews 8:10; 10:16; c) Daniel 7:13-14; d) Daniel 2:44-45; e) Mark 1:15; Matthew 4:17; f) John 3:3, 16; g) Luke 17:20-21; h) Mathew 13:11, 19, 23, 24, 31-33, 44-46, 47; i) Matthew 13:24-30; 7:15; j) Romans 14:17; k) Luke 16:16; Matthew 11:12; l) Matthew 21:43; m) Matthew 23:36; 24:34; n) Hebrews 8:13; o) Daniel 12:4-9; p) Matthew 16:24; John 12:26; John 13:15; q) John 17:24; 14:3; r) John 10:10; s) Matthew 21:43: t) John 14:18-23; u) Matthew 28:20; Hebrews 13:5; v) Mark 1:8; Acts 1:5; w) Acts 2:33, 39; x) Acts 2:16-17, 32-33; Joel 2:28-29; y) Acts 2:1-6, 41; z) John 3:3-6; Acts 1:5; aa) 1 Corinthians 12:27; Romans 12:5; Ephesians 4:12; bb) Acts 17:6; cc) 1 Peter 2:4-10; Exodus 19:6; dd) Romans 8:31; Matthew 1:23; ee) Ezekiel 1:16; 10:10

7

Third Delivering Call

Around 1500 BC God called people of faith out of slavery to live free of the world's two-class system. A second call to faith was renewed with the coming of Jesus Christ. Both historic responses to God's guidance entered a functional demise as people became submissive to the rule of man.

Our Bible records these two calls to people of faith and their response. While the second call to experience the kingdom reign of God would never cease to be in the earth, another gathering of people of faith was prophesied. What is the third delivering call to live in freedom?

Gathering People of Faith

This third call is noted as a gathering of the "scattered" people of faith.[a] Jeremiah prophesied:

> *I will gather them from the remote parts of the earth…He who scattered Israel (people of faith) will gather…and keep…as a shepherd keeps his flock.* [b]

Once again, God would gather people of faith to live as free people in natural places. Keep in mind, Scripture refers to Israel as those who seek to follow God's insightful guidance.[c] This third call to respond to God's guidance and function as a nation was revealed in three incremental stages.

The delivering Reformation of the 1500s was a spiritual call that revealed people of faith could live free of perceptions that there is only one way to believe and worship. One declaration came from Martin Luther: "Every believer is a priest before God."[d] Faith is not a singular response to God.

People begin to discover a spiritual, mental, and emotional release from the restricting oversight of official priests who regulated life and assumed to be mediators between God and man. Newly printed Bibles helped people begin to live, assemble, and worship free of the restrictions of the official religious order.

While people and nations broke away from the established religious order, an assurance of God's favor in life remained a nagging question. People typically were told: "Do your best and at death you will find out."

Great Awakenings

The Great Awakening Revivals of the early 1700s revealed that sincere repentance allows us to feel God's cleansing presence and know His favor is with us. As people found release from the relentless sense of condemnation and their deteriorating mannerisms, they began to live as *"reborn from above."*[(e)]

Then the newly developing thirteen colonies in the New World broke free of the ruling upper-class and became "One Nation under God," similar to the thirteen tribes of the first gathering of people of faith.

Emboldened with a new sense of purpose and the freedom to self-govern, democracy (rule of the people) was birthed into a republic (constitutional law), as a Democratic Republic. The freedom emboldened a prosperous middle class society to arise, similar to the first 500 years of old Israel.

As people realized "God is with us," they pursued with vigor the vision of freely living, worshiping, and prospering. The freedom allowed God to inspire many new conveniences, modes of travel, and ways of communication. The quality of spiritual and natural life began improving everywhere. The emerging prosperity created prosperous middle class societies.

Research by British Economist Angus Maddison illustrated that until 1820, 94% of the world's population lived in abject poverty. By 2015, however, only 9.6% remained in abject poverty. As people of faith prosper, everyone benefits, just as God promised our faithful father Abraham.[f]

Then in the early 1900s, Spirit Baptisms began revealing an insight that exceeds a "feeling and knowing." Baptisms are times when the Spirit of God noticeably immerses us in His presence. These times can be overwhelming moments or quiet inspirational times when we receive and absorb insight, gifting, and anointing. These are invitations for us to personally interact with God.

The freeing Reformation revealed faith in God is not restricted to one belief system or mode of worship. The Great Awakening revivals revealed how serious repentance brings us into a rebirth of awareness, as we feel and know we are forgiven. Immersion experiences in God's Spirit revealed we can live daily in fellowship with God's presence.

While these three historical stages are recognized as three moves of God, we seem to overlook their connective significance. These three experiences progressively return us into what was lost in the Garden of Eden—intimacy with the presence of God.

The first phase brought deliverance from restricting and enslaving religious overlords. The second phase revealed an assurance of forgiveness, so we can live as reborn from above. The third revealed we can experience the presence of God often. These three phases progressively revealed God's desire for our personal interaction with His abiding presence that is among us.

Ezekiel's Vision

The Kingdom of God is functioning today as the enabling presence of God among us and in our midst. Again, the reign of God is not a utopian or perfect state, it is a developing reality. As we respond and become more Christ-like people, His presence with us becomes more evident.

The prophet Ezekiel shared a vision he saw that illustrated God's voice producing three insightful actions.[g] The first directive was to *"Call the scattered bones together,"* giving them a cohesive purpose as connected bones. Then, *"Cover the bones with flesh,"* showing God's purpose involves natural life. Then God said, *"Breathe the spirit of life into the valley,"* to inspire and equip them spiritually and naturally as an army with the ability to fight and defend themselves.

Did you notice how God's activities in Ezekiel's

vision relate to the revealing of the last 500 years? The Reformation revealed God's call to come together with purpose (bones). The Great Awakening revivals revealed God's purpose in our life includes natural experience (flesh). Spirit immersions invite us into a daily fellowship with the presence of God (spirit). Our heavenly Father is very inclusive!

We may ask, what is the armor of God? Scripture instructs us to

> *Put on the full armor of God, so that you will be able to stand firm against the schemes of the devil* (dividing accusations)...*with truth...righteousness...the gospel of peace... faith...salvation, and the sword of the Spirit, which is the word of God.*[h]

The armor of people of faith is godly attitudes, expressions, and actions.

As individuals and gathering people, we can know and experience God within and without religious systems. As repentant people, in every society and nation, we can experience a rebirthing awareness of God's forgiving favor and experience life enhancing immersions in His presence.

This call to faith really is to "whosoever will" in our various cultures and nations. As people of faith today, one of our main problems is that we hesitantly respond to God's guidance because we fail to recognize how realistically His kingdom reign is actually functioning among our natural lives. Rather than wait for a someday, we want to wake-up and consciously partake of this reality.

1500 BC – God frees people to live under His guidance. Personal interaction is refused.

00 AD – God-in-Christ calls people of faith into personal interaction with God's presence.

1500 AD – The Eternal One once again invites people of faith to live under His guidance.

Now, 500 years later, will we repeat history and submit to the enslaving captivity of the two-class system? The "freedom to live, worship, and prosper with liberty and justice for all" is a God-given vision!

a) Isaiah 43:5-7; 56:8; b) Jeremiah 31:1, 8, 10; c) Romans 4:9-16; Galatians 3:6-9; d) Exodus 19:6; 1 Peter 2:5, 9-10; e) John 3:3; Ephesians 2:1; f) Genesis 22:18; Galatians 3:8; g) Ezekiel 37:1-14; h) Ephesians 6:11-17

8

Visionary People

When we receive spiritual, mental, and emotional releases from strict oversight, we can perceive and see more clearly. As a mid-day sun adds to the morning dawn, all revealing insight should prepare us for new awareness. Previous insights can be relevant if they do not restrict more light.

Visionaries not only see and perceive beyond current situations and circumstances, they often work through the complicated details of making the vision a reality. We recognize visionaries as explorers, discoverers, inventors, entrepreneurs, reformers, even parents who create and nurture. So, are we visionary people of faith?

God's Presence

God declared His vision for people of faith is a developing reality.

> *Behold, the tabernacle of God is among men, and He shall dwell among them, and they shall be His people, and God Himself shall be among them...the first things have passed away... Behold, I am making all things new."* [a]

This text notes three times that God's presence is "among us."

God's reign is not confined to one people, religious approach, or nation, but is experienced in part and at times, by all who seek to *do the right thing.*[b] The vision God gives for people of faith is inclusive, an improving reality that allows various responses, even times of doubt.

Jesus described the function of God's kingdom in the earth as allowing for different types of responses. We can be "shallow, joyful, worrisome, and fruitful."[c] God's rule among us allows for *tares among wheat, yeast among flour, hidden treasures, both good and bad fish.*[d] There are even *goats among sheep, wolves clothed as sheep, and people building on sand.*[e] God's kingdom in this earth is not a utopian state but includes a variety of variables. The presence of God is among us, assisting our maturing process!

Too often we complicate the truth of God's presence with us by saying it is either natural or spiritual. We are created and birthed into this life as natural people with spirit,[f] offspring of God and man. We are intended to mature as responsive children, spiritually and naturally.

God loves all of His offspring even when we ignore Him, are hesitant to hear His voice, stray from His guidance, respond as silly children, or are not religious. His desire is that we see and pursue His vision of a better life today and not passively wait for a someday, or an after-life.

Faith and Light

It is important to realize faith is more than believing. Faith is our active response to what God is saying and doing. We do not want to be complacent and wait for God to achieve things without our involvement. People of faith willingly respond and actively pursue God's vision for life.

We want to remember, *"Faith without works is useless...is dead."*[g] Faith involves our active participation. Scripture tells us to *"work out your salvation* (into daily life)...*for it is God who is at work in you."*[h] Our imperfect responses and improving adjustments help make God's vision for us a reality.

Gathered people of faith are called *"The Mountain of the Lord,"*[i] *"the light of the world...a city set on a hill,"*[j] and are to *"appear as lights in the world."*[k] Remember that

> *You are a chosen race, a royal priesthood, a holy nation, a people for God's own possession, so that you may proclaim the excellences of*

Him who has called you out of darkness into His marvelous light.[l]

Jesus encouraged us to *"Let your light shine (where?) before men (how?) in such a way that they may see your good works, and glorify your Father."*[m] God desires us, as responsive children, to be proactive in our limitations and imperfection: *"Arise and shine for the glory of the Lord has risen upon thee...the Lord will rise upon you and His glory will appear upon you."*[n]

Fresh insight into God's freeing and enabling vision actually enables us to receive additional experiences of His inspirational and influential oversight. God calls us to respond beyond our individuality with a vision as groups, communities, and nations. Together, we can experience "greater works."[o]

When we share our light and discuss issues under a unifying vision, we are an overcoming force.[p] *"Who among you is wise...let him show by his good behavior...the wisdom from above is first pure, then peaceable, gentle, reasonable, full of mercy and good fruits."*[q]

As the light of our personal and gathered lives shines brighter and brighter, darkness is dispelled and the destructive forces that seek to divide and captivate us lose their control.[r]

Freedom to Live, Worship, and Prosper

When the vision of living together under God's guidance is ignored or forgotten, the strength in our gatherings are weakened and can eventually be dismantled.[s] We want to proactively choose to continue under God's guidance as a free people. To do so, we must teach our children to refuse the deception that wants to take care of us and eventually enslave us.

We want to be involved enough to counter the bad policies that are introduced into the group, lest we contribute to delaying the blessings God desires to give. *"It was for freedom that Christ set us free; therefore keep standing firm and do not be subject again to a yoke of slavery."*[t]

The "freedom to live, worship and prosper with liberty and justice for all" is a God-given vision. While many do not realize the Kingdom of God is a spiritual and physical reality in the earth today, its reality is not negated. This vision began to revive 500 years ago as God began delivering, gathering, and anointing people all over the world. Many people and nations today shine as liberating lights.

Let us not repeat the previous patterns of ignoring or slipping away from God's guidance! We want to purposely live in the reality that God is with us, among us, and in our midst. Living conditions all over the world can continue to improve, despite the persistent destructive efforts of the ideologies of Fascism, Socialism, Communism, Globalism, and career politicians.

We are still free to respond to God's guidance as individuals, communities, states, and nations. This is a peaceful way to counter the efforts of all subversive activity that is bent on dividing our gatherings and destroying our God-inspired strength to arise and shine as fellowships and nations.

Rather than voting for the most likeable personality, can we focus and vote on the relevant issues and policies that affect the quality of our lives? Can we cast our vote and choose the best option? May we respond to God's vision for life and impact our world for the better!

a) Revelations 21:3-5; b) Hebrews 10:24; Romans 7:12; c) Matthew 13:18-23; d) Matthew 13:24-55; e) Matthew 25:32; 7:15, 24-27; f) Genesis 1:26; 2:7; Ecclesiastes 12:7 g) James 2:20, 26; h) Philippians 2:12-13; i) Isaiah 2:3; Micah 4:2; j) Matthew 5:14; k) Philippians 2:12-15; Proverbs 4:18-19; l) 1 Peter 2:9-10; m) Matthew 5:16; n) Isaiah 60:1-3; o) John 14:12; p) Isaiah 1:18; 43:26; q) James 3:13-17; r) Ephesians 6:12; s) Proverbs 29:18; t) Galatians 5:1

9

Full of God's Glory

We all long for God-in-Christ to become more obvious in the earth. While we sense His interaction in our lives, we desire more. Righteousness dispels evil's destruction and improves life in this world. Scripture says there will be a time when *"The earth will be filled with the knowledge of the glory of the Lord."*[a]

A knowledge of God does not mean everyone is responding to God's guidance. The Hebrew word that is translated *glory* refers to a visible display that the natural eye can see. Many are just observing the side effects of His reign or are partaking of its spillover benefits. So, when is the earth full of God's glory?

More than Spiritual

While no one has seen God with the natural eye, the invisible One is revealed in the life of Jesus Christ[b] and in responsive sons.[c] Aspects of God's glory are demonstrated by people of faith as they interact and illustrate elements of God's character, attitude, and personality (CAP). Since the days of Jesus, responders to God's guidance have been a visible illustration that Scripture calls, *"the Body of Christ."*[(d)]

Beyond the life of Jesus and the actions of our lives, many have seen visible evidence of God's reality. He is seen and heard: as angelic messengers,[(e)] an audible voice,[(f)] a felt presence,[(g)] and in dreams and visions.[(h)]

Our imperfect lives and gatherings that seek to do the right thing are visual witnesses the natural eye can observe. While God's Kingdom (governing influence) in the earth has never been a perfect function, *"The path of the righteous is like the light of dawn that shines brighter and brighter."*[(i)] We can be better!

Jesus encouraged us to: *"Let your light shine,* (where?) *before man,* (how?) *in such a way that they may see your good works, and glorify your Father."*[(j)] God is glorified in our obedient response to His guidance. He declares to people of faith: *"Arise and shine for the 'glory of the Lord has risen upon thee'... and 'His glory will appear upon you.' Nations will come to your light...to the brightness of your rising."*[(k)]

Ever since the days of Jesus, the Kingdom of God has been an experienced reality. The presence of God-in-Christ among us infuses spiritual realities that affect our natural lives. People and nations that are free to live, worship, and prosper become visible testaments that bring glory to God.[l]

All who respond to the influencing presence of God-in-Christ partake of His Kingdom reign spiritually and naturally. While many tend to divide God's purpose in our life as being either spiritual or natural, the truth is it begins as a spiritual awakening and is worked out in natural life.[p] God's reign in our life is never just spiritual; it is to become visibly evident in our natural life, as individuals and as gathered people.

Free to Live

While this is not proclaimed often, Paul emphasized its reality: *"Now may the God of peace Himself sanctify* (cleanse, make uncommon) *you entirely* (within and without); *may your spirit* (zoe-life) *and soul* (consciousness) *and body* (bios-natural life) *be preserved complete* (intact), *without blame at the coming* (in the presence) *of our Lord Jesus Christ."*[m]

During man's beginnings, an erroneous idea was accepted that indicates if we ignore God, *"you will be like God."*[n] This idea formed the fallen world order. The idea that I am like God began forming the two-class system with rulers. It is maintained

55

by the destructive forces of slander that produce fear in the ruled.

The Old and New Testaments give details of the two times God delivered people out of the two-class system, to live freely as a people of faith. Both eventually came up short as they summited to the rule of overlords. In the freeing Reformation of the 1500s, God intervened afresh, to deliver people from the two-class world order. Eventually this renewed freedom separated many nations from kingships.

The freedom to "live, worship, and prosper, with liberty and justice for all" is a God-given vision for people of faith. Since the mid-1800s, this freedom has produced visible evidence of God's presence among us. As testaments of God's blessings, new products and services have been created to improve living conditions.

Dividing Controls

However, in the mid-1800s, men who prefer to be in control began to combat this God-inspired freedom and promote what became known as Socialism. As the idea developed, it morphed into the forced rule of Communism. The idea seeks to ignore God and re-establish credibility to the crumbling two-class system.

The ideas of Lenin and Marx pitted workers against employers under the guise of equality for all. Where this system functions today, ruling authorities squash free enterprise and stifle free commerce to keep people from improving and prospering. Those in charge become as dictators and live above the underclass.

Until the mid-1800s, people were recognized by their different cultures and religions. Power seekers began to divide people by race to indicate one flesh is superior to another. Hitler said Germans were a superior race, and Mussolini claimed it of Italians. Race is still used today as a social and political tool to divide us.

Now 500 years after the Reformation began, God's historical call into freedom is being assaulted on multiple levels. The ideology of "man in control" inspires much of today's governmental politics, high-tech monopolies, and news platforms. We are bombarded with racial and economic divisions that seek to create or maintain discord. Hate and fear always divide and weaken us as families and as nations.

When people assume they are in charge, they generally wreak havoc in the lives of others. These forces of control are not a coordinated conspiracy; they just ascribe to the same ideology: "I can control and be in charge." When we give up or sur-render our liberties, we allow degrees of enslave-ment to be established.

A cancel culture can thrive if we unwittingly lend support to the ways of darkness and allow it to control and maintain enslaving rule over us. Whenever we try to appease or submit to intimi-dation with silence, we give opportunity, consent, and permission to destructive activity. We must let our revealing light shine!

We need to stop waiting for supernatural inter-vention and become involved. Light overcomes darkness[o] as we respond to God's leading guid-ance. As we consciously accept God's reign, we actually work out what God is working into us.[p] When our faith is obvious, its visible quality spills into communities, states, and countries. As the many membered Body of Christ[q] is responsive, God is visibly glorified in the earth.

Let's stand against the controlling efforts of class division and stand up for the freedom God has provided. While some fail to recognize how fully the Kingdom of God functions in our life as a spiritual and natural reality, it does not negate its reality. His reigning influence in our life includes our full being. It has an affect on nations all over the world. The glory of the Lord is shining and becoming more visible on the earth.

a) Habakkuk 2:14; b) John 1:18; 14:9; c) Genesis 1:26; John 14:3; 1 John 4:12; d) Ephesians 4:12-16; Romans 12:1-5; 1 Corinthians 12:12-27; e) Hebrews 1:13-14; Psalm 91:11; f) Exodus 3:2-4; Deuteronomy 4:11-12; Acts 9:3-7; g) 1 Kings 6:13; Luke 24:13-15; h) Acts 2:14-17; Daniel 2:28; 7:1; Job 7:14; i) Proverbs 4:18; j) Matthew 5:16; k) Isaiah 60:1-3; l) 2 Corinthians 3:2-4; m) 1 Thessalonians 5:23; n) Genesis 3:4; o) John 1:4-5; Ephesians 5:8-10; p) Philippians 2:12-13; q) Romans 12:1-5

10

Here or Yet To Come

There are many perceptions regarding the return of Jesus Christ. Some are anticipating an antichrist to appear and make life worse before Jesus returns. Many expect Jesus to come as a naturally visible person, force God's will on everyone, and institute a utopian reign of God.

Yet, many sense they are experiencing the presence of Jesus today as the enabling presence of God that is with us, among us, and in our midst. So, is Jesus already here or is He yet to come?

God's Abiding Presence

When this natural realm began, God spoke and His expressive word created this ever expanding universe with its "heavens and earth." [a] Millenniums later, two thousand years ago now, God spoke and His expressive word impregnated the virgin Mary. This began forming the baby Jesus, who was to be known as *"Immanuel, which means 'God with us.'"* [b]

Just before the three-year ministry of Jesus, John the Baptist called people to repent and display their decision by being baptized in water. The Greek word translated *baptize* means immerse. John proclaimed Jesus is *"the one who baptizes* (immerses) *in/with Holy Spirit."*[c] For three years Jesus was seen and known as Christ (the anointed one). God was clearly with Him!

Jesus told His followers: *"After a little while the world will behold me no more; but you will behold me."*[d] How would this be? After the death and resurrection, perceptions of Jesus began to change. Rather than God's anointed one, Jesus was now appearing as a presence of Spirit!

Before the crucifixion, Jesus declared: *"I will never desert you, nor...forsake you,"*[e] He also proclaimed: *"My Father will love...and 'We' will come...and make 'our' abode...the Helper, the Holy Spirit."*[f] The Holy Spirit is one of the three expressive personalities of the Eternal One.

Forty days after the resurrection, Jesus appeared to leave by ascending out of natural sight. By leaving their ability to see with natural eyes, the spoken word of God that became Jesus, appeared to go away. Angels declared on that day: *"He...will come in just the same way as you have watched him go,"* as a spiritual presence.[g]

The spoken word of God that became the personage of Jesus, would again function *"with the glory which I had with You* (Father) *before the world was,"* [(h)] as God's expressive word. The same presence returned a few days after the ascension as the baptizing presence of *"the Father and the Son."* [(i)]

The spoken expression of God returned to be with responders as a presence of the Father and Son. While we do not see Jesus with natural eyes, our spiritual senses can see and experience His expressions.

Understanding Presence

Peter explained to observers on that Day of Pentecost that they were witnessing what God promised through Joel: *"God says…I will pour forth of My Spirit upon all mankind…I will in those days pour forth of My Spirit."* [(j)] On that day in Jerusalem, as a very visible illustration, Jesus immersed over 3,000 people in God's presence. [(k)] What a delight to know the expression of God, that became the man Jesus, returns to us as Holy Spirit, to immerse us in the Eternal One's presence.

Since that Day of Pentecost, the expression of God that we know as Jesus, has been with and among us as the Holy Spirit! Saul, who became Paul, persecuted followers of the presence of Jesus until a great light appeared and a Voice said: *"I am Jesus whom you are persecuting."*[l] Jesus spoke to Paul as the expressive Voice of God, to change his perception of God and His ways.[m]

Paul later declared: *"We have known Christ according to the flesh, yet now we know him thus* (in this way) *no longer."*[n] Paul's declaration was not just for that day, it was for all time.

It is easier to grasp this when we realize the Greek *parousia* is a combination of *para* which means "near, with" and *eimi*, which means "to be." *Parousia* means "to be near with" as a presence. Along with several Greek words, it is translated as "coming." This confuses rather than enlightens.

Translators however had to translate it accurately twice. Once of Paul: *"his personal 'presence' is unimpressive and his speech contemptible,"*[o] and once by Paul who said: *"not in my 'presence' only, but now much more in my absence."*[p]

Affirming clarity comes when parousia is translated as "presence" instead of "coming." *"Strengthen your hearts, for the 'presence' of the Lord is at hand."*[q]

"He who is 'present' will come (Greek *heko*, has come)."[r]

"We made (make) *known to you the power and 'presence' of our Lord Jesus Christ."*[s]

"That lawless one will be (is) *revealed...by the appearance of His 'presence.'"*[t]

"What will be the sign of your 'presence,' and of the end of the age (these times)*?"*[u]

"In the presence (Greek – in front) *of our Lord Jesus at his 'presence.'"*[v]

We should also note, the word *second* is linked to the return of Jesus only once: *"So Christ also, having been offered once to bear the sins of many, shall appear a second time for salvation, without reference to sin, to those who 'eagerly await'* (Greek – look for) *him."* [w] The second coming of Jesus is as God's Holy Spirit, to assist our transformation into mature expressions of God. We should look for Jesus to be with us as God's abiding, gifting, anointing, and healing presence.

The Revelation of Jesus

In those early days, it was difficult for many to receive the revelation that Jesus was functioning as the enlightening and anointing presence of "Immanuel, God with us." The multitudes who saw Jesus as the anointed One found it hard to accept Jesus as the expressive presence of God's Spirit.

The Kingdom of God's reign is not something the natural eye is able to observe.[x] However, some believers in New Testament times, like today, wanted a physical return of Jesus to forcefully establish a natural style kingdom reign in the earth. Those who did not understand asked: *"Where is the promise of His presence* (parousia) *for...all continues just as it was from the beginning?"*[y]

John began his book of Revelation by addressing the issue, announcing, this is *"The revelation of Jesus Christ."* John also acknowledged the angel who spoke with him was *"Jesus Christ...the first-born from the dead."*[z] Additionally, John stated the Voice that spoke was *"The Lord God, who is and was and is 'to come'* (Greek – *erchomai,* coming)."[aa] John's book finishes with *"Yes, I am coming quickly."*[bb] The presence of Jesus as the presence of God with us is not delayed; He comes!

Instead of waiting for Jesus to come, we want to realize how fully Jesus, as God-in-Christ, is with us today. He is among us and in our midst as God's expressive presence, the Holy Spirit. As the spoken expression of God, Jesus wants to *"write His Laws in our minds and on our hearts."*[cc]

As the presence of God, Jesus heals our sickness, feeds our hunger, satisfies our thirst, strengthens our weakness, embraces our unloveliness, and delivers us from enslavement. He is with us to assist our transformation into better images and likenesses of God's character, attitude, and personality.

God is one and His three expressive personalities (Father, Son, and Holy Spirit) come from the presence of the Eternal One. Thankfully, God is not limited by our perceptions, by our approach to Him, or by any other visual we may have. As we call on God, He listens to the intent of our heart.

May this reality encourage and empower each of us to arise and be all God desires us to be—personally and as nations!

a) John 1:1-4; 2 Corinthians 4:6; Genesis 1:1-3; b) Matthew 1:18-22; John 1:14; Like 1:30, 35; Matthew 1:20-21; c) John 1:33; Mark 1:8; d) John 14:19; e) Hebrews 13:5; f) John 14:23-26; g) Acts 1:11; h) John 17:5; John 1:1-4, 14; i) Acts 2:1-7, 32-33; John 14:9-11; j) Acts 2:17-18; k) Acts 2:33, 41; l) Acts 9:3-7, 17-18; 26:14-15; m) Galatians 1:11-18; n) 2 Corinthians 5:16; o) 2 Corinthians 10:10; p) Philippians 2:12; q) James 5:8; r) Hebrews 10:37; Matthew 11:3; s) 2 Peter 1:16; t) 2 Thessalonians 2:8; u) Matthew 24:3; v) 1 Thessalonians 2:19; w) Hebrews 9:28; x) Luke 17:20; y) 2 Peter 3:4; z) Revelations 1:2-6; aa) Revelations 1:8; bb) Revelations 22:20; cc) Hebrews 8:10, 13; 10:16

11

End of Days

We often hear the phrases: "These are the end times," "We are in the last days," and "The end is near." Much fear is generated based on the scriptural last days, proclaiming disastrous times. Books and movies portray a coming doomsday as a time of tribulation and destruction.

The assertions usually apply to a large range of reasons: a sinful nation, an ungodly world, a cold and fruitless religion, and a wayward generation. Many Bible teachers support such thoughts so we want to know, when are the scriptural end times and are we actually in them? Let's examine Scripture and discover when it says the end of days actually will happen.

Understanding Time

As we begin our search, it is helpful to understand time. When God created the natural universe, the cycles of time began.[a] Days come and go as one passes and another arrives. A multitude of days are generally looked at as seasons, which also come and go. While history records days as twenty-four hour periods, we speak of the day as the time when light shines.

To be clear, everything in this natural realm experiences last times and an end of days. Our days are even filled with moments that begin and end. When we say "those days" or "the days to come," we repeat what Scripture calls "the former and latter days." The passage of days will continue as long as the natural realm exists. So an "end" is not an end of all time.

Our Old Testament translations alternate between the "last days" and "latter days." When Jacob gathered his sons to *"tell you what shall befall you in the last days,"*[b] he described the personality traits of each son and what their children's activity would be like. The NASB correctly translates the phrase as *"in the days to come."* Their last days were not their end.

The prophet Daniel spoke most about end times in scripture. During the first occasion, the angel Gabriel told of the end of the Babylon Empire, which was soon fulfilled by the Medes and Persians *"in the appointed time of the end."*[c] In the second event, the angel Michael spoke of the end of the Mede and Persian Empire, which fell to Greece *"in the latter days."*[d]

Daniel lived to see both ruling empires come to their end. While the people continued, their authority as dominant kingdoms ended.

"These Last Days"

Isaiah and Micah are two prophets that addressed "the last days." Both said: *"It will come about in the last days that the mountain of the house of the lord will be established as the chief of the mountains."*[e] In Scripture, prophetic mountains usually depict nations and kingdoms.[f] In comparison to the days of these mountains, God's kingdom would be dominant in the last days.

In the midst of his book, Daniel tells of the coming of *"One like the son of man...his dominion ...will not pass away...will not be destroyed."*[g] This promised Messiah would introduce a new Kingdom reality that would never end. Daniel proclaimed that all who partook of the new kingdom *"will awake...will shine as the stars of heaven...and lead many to righteousness."*[h]

The *"One like the son of man"* was Jesus Christ. He simplified the Law of Moses, just as God did, into an easy and insightful perception: *"You shall love the Lord your God with all your heart...soul...and mind... and your neighbor as yourself...on these two commandments depend the whole Law and the*

Prophets."[i] The purpose of the Law became so clear even the uneducated could easily pursue its reality.

The last chapter of Daniel's book speaks of *"the end"* four times, *"until the end of time"* twice, once as the *"end of these wonders"* and the *"end of the age."*[j] Each of these indicates a future beyond Daniel's days. This chapter speaks of *"the shattering the power of the holy people."*[k]

Who were considered to be the holy people? They were people of faith that subscribed to the Law of Moses.

Old Testament End Times

Jesus described Daniel's end time as a transfer, saying: *"Therefore I say to you, the kingdom of God will be taken away from you, and be given to a nation* (peoples) *producing the fruit of it."*[l]

The Apostle Paul acknowledged this reality was happening in his day: *"But you, brethren, are not in darkness…for you are all sons of light and sons of day…so then let us not sleep as others do, but let us be alert and sober."*[m] Again, *"For this reason it says, 'Awake, sleeper, and arise from the dead, and Christ will shine on you.'"*[n]

He went on to declare this terrible end time distress would come during that very generation: *"All these things shall come on this generation,"* amplifying, *"This generation will not pass away until all these things take place."*[o] The end of Judaism's oversight climaxed in 70 AD with the destruction of their historical seats of authority, Jerusalem and the Holy Temple.[p]

Peter, Paul, and John each acknowledged they were living in the end times of Daniel's last chapter: *"For He was foreknown before the foundation of the world, but has appeared in these last times."*[q] *"God...in these last days has spoken to us in His Son."*[r] *"Children, it is the last hour...we know that it is the last hour."*[s]

The Old Testament prophets spoke of the end, last, and latter days as historical seasons for authoritative ruling powers. Daniel lived to see two of them. The third would come in the future when Jewish oversight of the people of faith was to end.

At that time and in those days, God would gather people of faith to Himself instead of the Old Covenant, which had become a religious system. At that time, in those days, God's ways would be *"written in their minds and on their hearts."*[t]

Now, 2000 years ago, during the fulfillment of

Daniel's last days, *"One like the son of man"* changed the perception of God's kingdom in the earth. Jesus introduced the reality that we can have a more personal relationship with God as our loving and insightful Father. This new reality would not end but would continue until its glory filled the whole earth.[u]

This is not all Scripture says about the last days or end of time. In the next chapter we will examine the New Testament applications that speak of more than past historical end times.

a) Genesis 1:1-5; b) Genesis 49:1, KJV; c) Daniel 8:17-20, 23; d) Daniel 10:13-14, 20; 11:29, 35, 40; e) Isaiah 2:2; Micah 4:1; f) Daniel 2:35; g) Daniel 7:13-14; h) Daniel 12:2-3; i) Matthew 22:37-40; Deuteronomy 6:5; 10:12 j) Daniel 12:4, 6, 9, 15; k) Daniel 12:7; l) Matthew 21:43; m) 1 Thessalonians 5:4-6; n) Ephesians 5:14; o) Matthew 23:26; 24:34; p) Daniel 9:24-27; q) 1 Peter 1:20; 4:7; r) Hebrews 1:1-2; s) 1 John 2:18; t) Jeremiah 31:31-33; Hebrews 8:7-13; 12:22-24; u) Numbers 14:21; Luke 1:33

12

Our Last Times

God declared many times that this created natural universe with its time cycles will not come to an end or cease to function.[a] While this natural universe and our earth exists, time will continue. The phrase, *"There should be time no longer,"* only appears in the KJV once. Later translations correctly say: *"There shall be no delay."*[b] Time will not cease as long as the natural realm exists.

Scripture declares, *"There is an appointed time for everything...for every event under heaven."*[c] Everything in this life experiences their appointed time. All seasons have beginnings and endings as a course of natural life. So, are we currently experiencing our last times?

Three Historical End Times

As our last chapter points out, the Old Testament end of days speak of three historical end times. Two were fulfilled in Daniel's lifetime as the ruling Babylon and the Mede/Persian empires came to their end. The third prophesied end of days that would come in a future time. The system that came out of the first Covenant and ruled over the "holy people" would also see its end times.[d]

During this third end times, Jesus Christ began to redefine perceptions of God's kingdom. The reign of God came to be known as personal relationships with God-in-Christ. It was more than an earthly kingdom with the limitations of a natural location.[e] This greater reality would never end and would eventually fill the whole earth.[f]

Following the days when Jesus walked the earth, God gathered people into His kingdom reign by means of a New Covenant. The focus was not on keeping a Law or making annual sacrifices for bad behavior, nor gathering into one earthly area.

The introduction of the New Covenant amplified God's forgiveness is received by our repentant efforts to change. Our interaction with God's abiding presence would allow Him to write His insightful ways *"in minds and on hearts."*[g]

The Great Tribulation

Jesus Christ announced to His generation that: *"The time is fulfilled, and the kingdom of God is at hand"* (readily available).[h] He also proclaimed to the religious authorities: *"The Kingdom of God will be taken away from you and given to a nation* (Greek *ethnos* – gathered people) *producing the fruit of it."* [i]

Jesus then spoke of *"a great tribulation"* that was coming *"upon this generation."* [j] The foretold great tribulation was historically experienced in 70 AD with the long siege and destruction of the city of Jerusalem and the Holy Temple. [k]

Those last times of the old order were affirmed by Peter, John, and Paul, who also spoke of *"these last days/times/hour."* [l] Paul further affirmed the end times was in full swing; *"When the fullness of time came, God sent forth His son, born of a woman,"* [m] and *"upon whom the ends of the ages have come."* [n] Peter also confirmed *"He was foreknown...but has appeared in these last times,"* [o] and *"the end of all things is at hand."* [p]

History records the time before the change, Jesus brought as BC (Before Christ). The ages of time that followed are called AD (Latin: *Anno Domini*) and are commonly referred to as "After Jesus." The New Testament records the seasonal ending of the Old Covenant as a time of great tribulation. It also records the New Covenant season as a reality that would never end.

Staying Faithful Until The End

Our Bibles bounce between the terms "latter days," "last days," and "end times." In the Greek language of the New Testament, the words "end, latter, and last" (Greek – *telos*) actually mean: outcome; conclusion of the matter, experience, or season. As we look further into how the New Testament uses the terms, we find they also speak of the end of our personal life in this world.

While each of the following quotes apply to the generation of Jesus, they also address our personal lives as we grow old. *"In the last days, difficult times will come,"*[q] and *"the one who has endured to the end will be saved."*[r] *"He who keeps My deeds to the end"*[s] and *"If we hold fast our confidence…firm to the end."*[t] Even, *"Having been freed from sin…you derive your benefit…and the outcome* (end), *eternal life."*[u]

At least three times Jesus said: *"I myself will raise him up on the last day."*[v] Each time, He spoke of our individual physical death as our last day. When our life in this world ends, we consciously exit the natural sphere and fully enter the realm of eternity, *"for a salvation ready to be revealed in the last time."*[w] When our physical life ends, our conscious awareness enters and begins to experience a fuller salvation that is void of natural complications.

Each of the Old Testament last days and end times have come and gone. While the New Testament talks about "these end times and days," it also speaks of our future "end of time" when our personal life ceases, and we enter eternity. We are encouraged to stay faithful to our earthly end.

While Jesus said *"The word I spoke is what will judge him at the last day,"*[x] we must remember God's judgments are always corrective measures.[y] While God condemns bad intentions, ill behavior, and erroneous actions, He does not condemn people. He seeks to correct our corrupt perceptions by improving our thoughts, redirecting our desires and behavior to improve our maturing experience. *"The judgments of the Lord are true; they are righteous altogether."*[z]

Scripture speaks of our salvation (from sinful ways) as a reality we begin to know during this life.[aa] We can daily sense eternal perceptions of God-Light and feel experiences God-Love. We can even become better expressions of God's heart.

a) Genesis 8:20-22; Jeremiah 33:20, 25; Ecclesiastes 1:1-11; Psalm 104:5; 2 Peter 3:3; b) Revelation 10:6; c) Ecclesiastes 3:1; d) Daniel 12:7; e) John 18:36; Luke 17:20-21; f) Numbers 14:21; Luke 1:33; g) Jeremiah 31:31-33; Hebrews 8:7-13; 12:22-24; h) Matthew 3:2; 4:17; 10:7; Mark 1:15; i) Matthew 21:43; j) Matthew 24:21, 34; 23:36; Luke 21:9; k) Matthew 3:2; 4:17; 10:7; l) 1 Peter 1:5, 20; 1 John 2:18; Romans 13:11; Hebrews

1:2; m) Galatians 4:4; n) 1 Corinthians 10:11; o) 1 Peter 1:20; p) Peter 4:7, 17; q) 2 Timothy 3:1; r) Matthew 10:22; 24:13-14; Mark 13:13; s) Revelations 2:26; t) Hebrews 3:6, 14; 6:11; u) Romans 6:22; v) John 6:40, 44, 54; 11:24; w) 1 Peter 1:5; x) John 12:48; y) Hebrews 12:5-11; Proverbs 3:12; z) Psalms 19:9; aa) John 5:24; 6:47

About the Author

 At nine years of age, Keith dedicated his life to God and in his pre-teen years became a strong student of the Scriptures. Rather than just believe, the prayer of his heart was "Lord, I want to understand all You want to reveal." It has been and remains an exciting and insightful journey.

To contact Keith Carroll by email:
keith@RelationalGospel.com
or write to: Keith Carroll, PO Box 341,
Newburg, PA 17240

Bi-Weekly Blog

Don't miss any of Keith's inspiring thoughts. In conjunction with his books, each blog focuses on insights that bring amazing clarity to Scripture, so we can more effectively apply eternal qualities to our daily lives. These encouraging posts are the ideal size for pondering, discussing, and helping you experience deeper intimacy with the presence of God—the Eternal One.

Sign up for his bi-weekly blog at
http://relationalgospel.com/

Other books by Keith Carroll

 Welcome to the culture of Christ: an environment filled with rich appreciation for the ways of God! *The Christ Culture* is a fresh way of looking at God's desire for our life on earth. This culture is an environment where God's inspiring presence is experienced and Christlike attitudes and behaviors are encouraged. Light is shed on the most important concepts of our faith walk.

Learn what are the "Ways of God," what are the seven processes of salvation, and why things happen as they do. How do God's methods of living bring us into His heart's desire?

Come on a life improving journey and explore the maturing ways of God among us. As we connect the dots, you'll receive new clarity about life. You'll see how to best apply the ways of God to your personal life so you more correctly reflect and resemble God.

"I have reviewed countless manuscripts over the past 30 years, but found few have had this clarity." —Don Nori Sr., founder, Destiny Publishers

The Christ Culture ISBN 978-0-9860923-1-2

Who am I? Why am I here? These questions have been pondered down through the ages! *Created to Relate* brings clarity and new insight into the design and function of the human body, soul, and spirit.

Discover the clear difference between what you are as a being and who you are as a person. Light is shed on how we are designed to function and the difference between our soul and spirit.

Keith's dissection of the human heart is ground-breaking. He unveils the mystery of life and how we live natural and spiritual lives, simultaneously. You are invited to embark on an exciting journey through Scripture and discover God's creative intention for your life. Learn the truth about what it means to be made in the image and likeness of the Eternal One.

"How we are designed to function and relate to God becomes clear, concise, and illuminating. This book is extremely helpful to all who want to walk in deeper intimacy with our creator."
—Catherine Zoller, speaker and author

Created to Relate ISBN 978-0-9860923-3-6

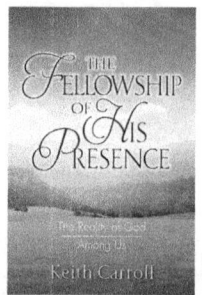

Can we actually hear God speak? Is intimacy with the Eternal One possible today? Yes, God invites each of us into *The Fellowship of His Presence*!

The Eternal One is not just a distant super Being who spins galaxies from His fingertips. His Fatherly heart loves us more than we can comprehend. Keith shares insights to bring amazing clarity to the Gospel message and shows there is no reason to wait for a second coming of Jesus—He is already "with us" as a presence of Spirit. The multi-faceted nature of God becomes clear. New light is shed on the tree of the knowledge of good and evil.

You'll discover how a fiction became an accepted theology, the antichrist is not a person, and when the biblical "last days" actually occurred. How do we mature into God's creative intention? Discover how we can interact with the Eternal One and live as Jesus did.

"Throughout these pages, it is clear that keeping Jesus and our fellowship with him at the forefront of all our doctrines and ideals is the most important thing we can do." —Sandra Querin, JD, MBA, Th.D., Pastor, The Revival Center, Clovis, CA

The Fellowship of His Presence ISBN 978-0-9860923-5-0

Additional Resources

Please visit:
http://relationalgospel.com
where you can find: Group Discussion Guides

Research has found that we retain 20% of what we hear, 50% of what we hear and see, 70% of what we discuss, and 90% of what we do. Our retention is greatly increased when insights are discussed. Friendly conversation helps enlarge everyone's understanding and can ease the application of new insights into our daily lives. To facilitate group discussions, chapter by chapter, we have put together a leader's resource packet for each of our books. Our guide includes these helpful resources:

- Tips on how to engage conversation in small groups
- Hand-outs with 12 to 14 discussion questions for each chapter
- Before and after participant evaluation forms

Our guide is a must-have resource to make your group experience more effective. Sizable discounts are available on orders of 6 or more copies of one title. As a bonus, we include, free of charge, this valuable guide as a professionally prepared pdf file.

www.ingramcontent.com/pod-product-compliance
Lightning Source LLC
Chambersburg PA
CBHW071112120626
46546CB00003B/1306